Published by:

Pietas Publications
Waynesboro, Virginia, USA
web: www.jasperburns.com
email: pietas@jasperburns.com

WHAT ANIMAL AM I?

By Jasper Burns

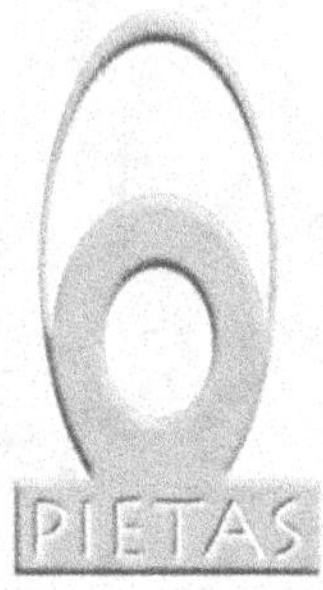

Copyright 2017

What Animal Am I?

How much do we know about the animals around us?

On the following pages are lists of interesting facts about different animals. Most are mammals, but there are also a few birds, reptiles, fish, and other creatures.

Most of these animals are familiar, but a few are less well-known.

After each list of facts is a picture of the animal it describes.

How many animals can you identify before looking at the pictures?

What animal am I?

- When I was born, I was no bigger than a pinto bean!

- My ancestors came from South America, but now we live as far north as Canada.

- My kind was living during the time of the dinosaurs.

- I eat all sorts of things, including grains, nuts, fruits, earthworms, eggs, birds, mice, snails, insects, and even frogs.

- I can have babies when I am not quite one year old.

- I have little pockets under my fur where my babies can hide and drink milk.

- I am most active during the nighttime.

- Sometimes, when I am cornered, I pretend that I am dead.

- I never hibernate, even when it is below zero degrees.

- I can hang from a branch by my tail!

OPOSSUM (with close-up of baby)

What animal am I?

- I can be almost 15 feet long and weigh over 1,400 pounds when full-grown.

- As an adult, I have no teeth.

- I am a superb swimmer, with speeds of over 50 miles per hour, and I can dive to depths of almost 10,000 feet!

- I am mature at age five and can live to be as much as 16 years old.

- I eat fish, including mackerels, herrings, bluefish, and rockfish. I also eat squid and crustaceans.

- I am solitary for the most part, but will sometimes form loosely-connected groups.

- Our largest females can carry as many as 29 million eggs at one time!

- I love to jump high out of the water and crash back into the waves. This may help me get rid of surface parasites.

- As an adult, my only predators are killer whales, mako sharks, and humans.

SWORDFISH

What animal am I?

- If possible, I like to migrate from lakes or the ocean into small streams to spawn.

- Depending on where I live, I can grow to weigh as much as 20 pounds.

- The largest of my kind ever caught weighed 48 pounds, but it had been genetically modified by humans.

- I am predatory and eat a wide variety of animal foods, including many types of fish and fish eggs, aquatic insects, and terrestrial insects that fall into the water.

- I will also eat dead fish.

- I am native to the area of the northern Pacific Ocean and its tributaries, from Russia to California.

- I have been introduced into rivers and lakes in many parts of the world.

- In the ocean, I eat squid and amphipods as well as fish.

- I am usually silver-blue in color with many dark spots and a reddish band running lengthwise on both sides of my body.

- When I am a juvenile, I have a series of large vertical, more or less oval dark spots on the sides of my body.

RAINBOW TROUT

What animal am I?

- I live in western North America in mountain conifer forests up to 13,000 feet.

- I move to lower elevations for the winter.

- I am mostly gray, with a white face and rump and mostly black wings.

- I am very noisy, with a harsh, ratcheting call.

- I have a long, sharply pointed bill.

- I eat seeds that I pry out of conifer cones with my bill. I gather many of these seeds together in caches for winter food.

- I also eat moths, beetles, crickets, grasshoppers, and ants as well as birds' eggs, nestlings, chipmunks, and even ground squirrels.

- Our mated pairs build nests together and take turns sitting on the eggs, even in snowstorms with sub-zero weather.

- Our two to six eggs are pale green with spots. We feed the nestlings with regurgitated pine seeds.

- I like to dive into canyons with my wings folded, then open my wings and pull up just before I crash.

- I can cling to tree trunks, looking for grubs under the bark.

NUTCRACKER

What animal am I?

- When I am full grown, I usually weigh less than half a pound.

- I am awake at night and asleep during the day.

- I can find my way home from almost anywhere.

- I eat lichens, fungi, nuts, seeds, insects, eggs, and baby birds.

- I am social in the winter but like to be alone or with just my family in the summer.

- I often eat upside down.

- When I chirp, I sound like a warbler.

- I like to live in old hollow trees or in attics.

- Owls and cats like to eat me.

- I can glide long distances.

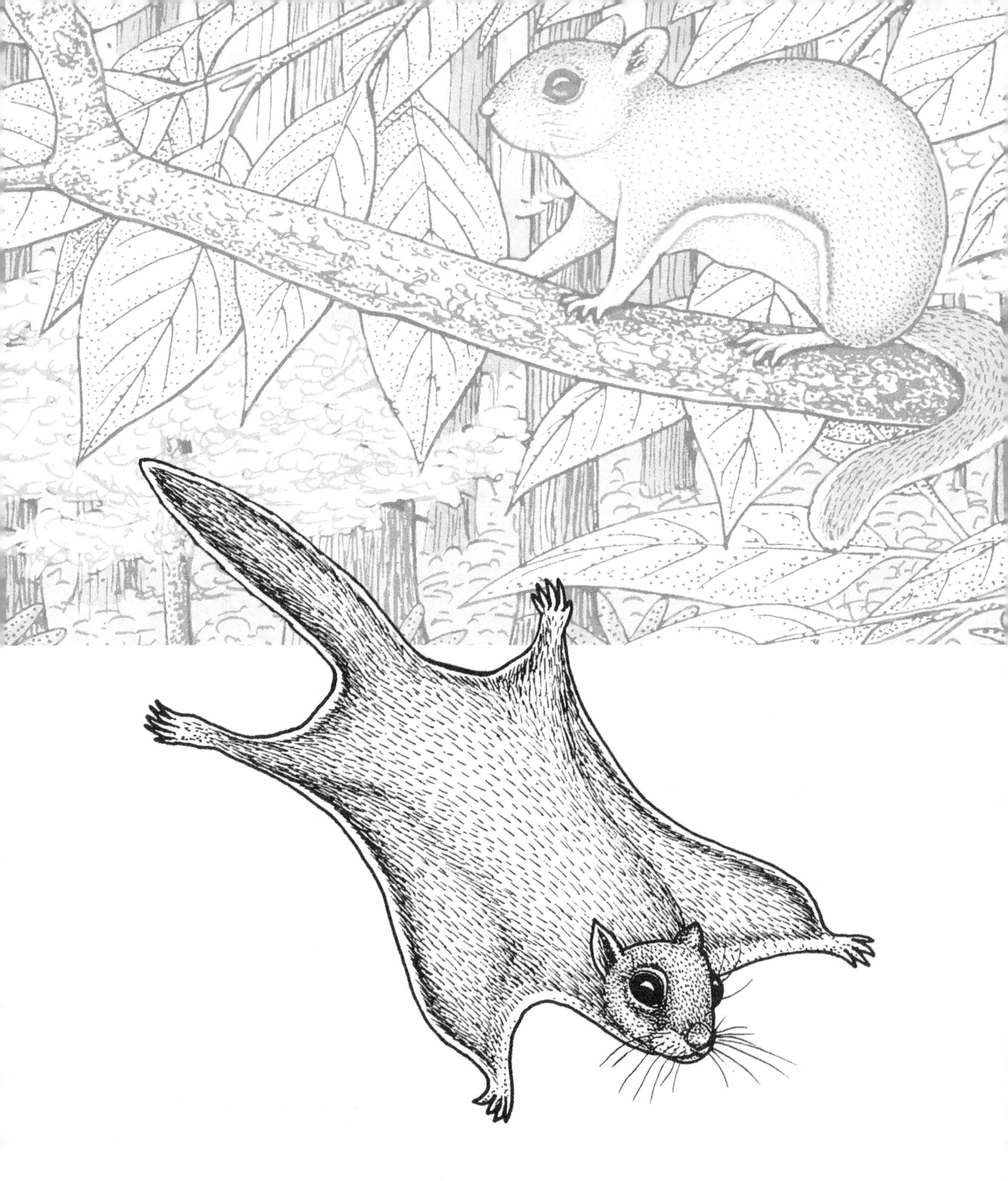

NORTHERN FLYING SQUIRREL

What animal am I?

- I weigh less than half an ounce when I am born.

- I eat acorns, nuts, pine and spruce cones and needles, fruits, berries, and mushrooms.

- I gather piles of pine cones and mushrooms so I'll know where to find food.

- I also eat birds' eggs and nestlings.

- I am very talkative and can be very loud.

- I am very active all year round.

- In the winter, I grow small tufts on my ears.

- In the summer, I build a nest with mosses, lichens, twigs, and shredded bark.

- Bobcats, house cats, martens, and owls like to eat me.

- I only live in the evergreen forests of the western United States and Canada.

CHICKAREE (DOUGLAS' SQUIRREL)

What animal am I?

- I make many sounds, including shrieks, squeals, and trills, and I purr when I am calm and happy.

- I eat birds, mice, eggs, insects, earthworms, rats, voles, chipmunks, shrews, and rabbits.

- Males of my species are twice as big as females.

- I am the most widespread mammalian carnivore in the Western Hemisphere.

- In northern parts of my range, I turn completely white in the winter – except for the very tip of my tail, which remains black.

- I like to live near water and am good at climbing trees.

- I am most active during the night, but I also like to chase voles during the day.

- I kill as many animals for food as I can find, then store the ones I can't eat right away for later meals.

- I mate in the middle of summer, and my babies are born in the spring.

- I reuse the dens made by other animals and make nests in them with the soft fur of animals that I eat.

- People insult each other by calling them by my name.

LONG-TAILED WEASEL

What animal am I?

- I always live near water and I am an excellent swimmer, moving as fast as six miles per hour.

- I can stay under water for up to 15 minutes.

- I am most active at night.

- Special toenails on my hind feet are used for combing my fur.

- I am mature and ready to leave my parents and find a mate when I am two years old.

- When I choose a mate, we stay together for life.

- I can grow to four feet long and weigh more than 80 pounds.

- Mounds of mud with deposits of scent from my anal glands mark my territory.

- Otters, wolves, coyotes, red foxes, and bobcats prey on me.

- Trees are my favorite food – especially maples, willows, aspens, poplars, and birches.

- People eat my meat and use my fur for clothing.

BEAVER

What animal am I?

- I like solitude but usually search for food with a partner.

- I have four nipples and usually have three or four young at a time.

- I travel south in the autumn and often hibernate during the winter.

- I am most active in the evening.

- Insects are my favorite food – especially beetles, ants, flies, moths, and leafhoppers.

- Sometimes I travel far out to sea, but I'm not a good swimmer.

- I am a rusty reddish-brown in color.

- Males of my species are brighter and richer in color than females.

- I usually roost in trees, but sometimes I do so in caves.

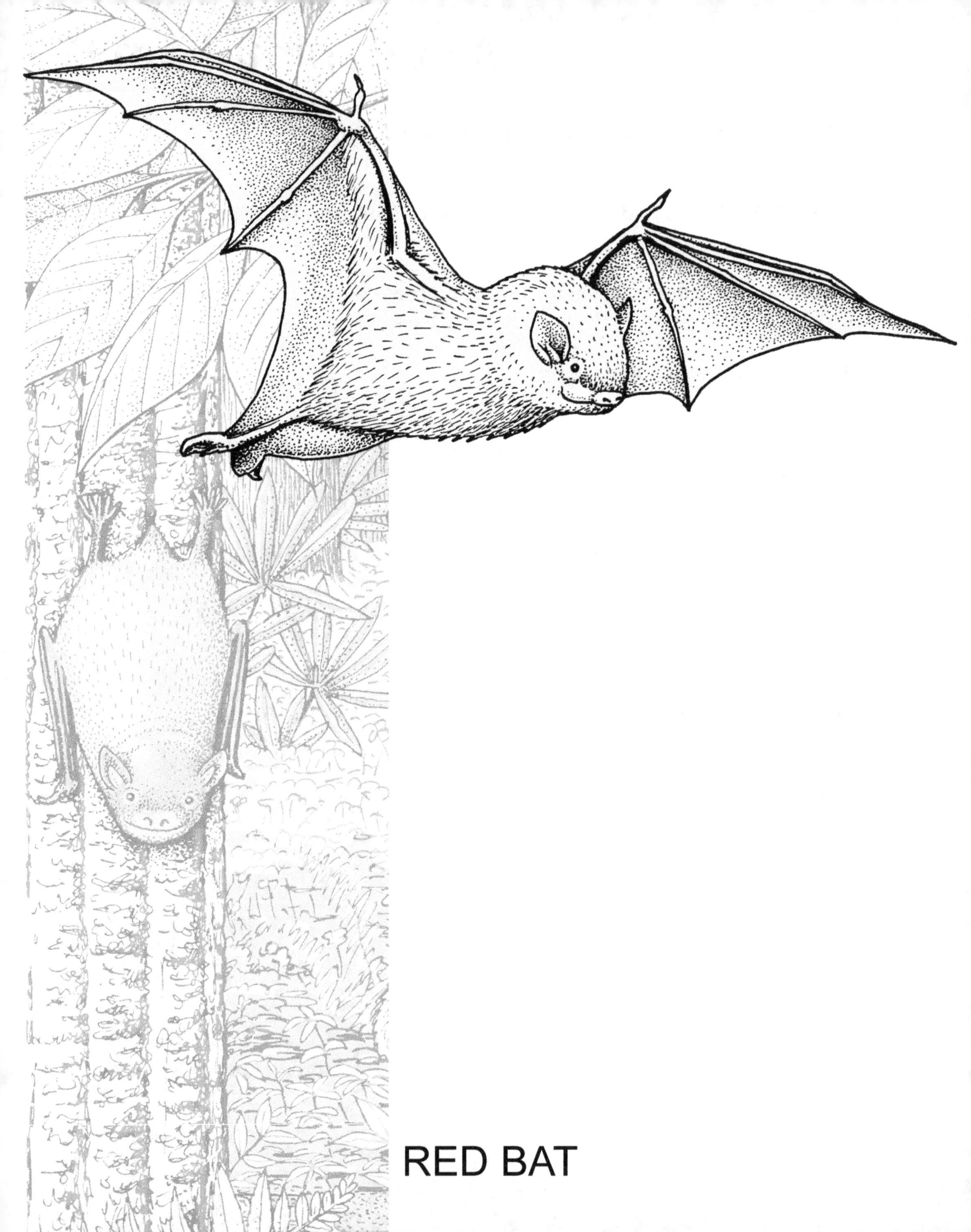

RED BAT

What animal am I?

- I can be as much as 8 ½ inches long, but am usually closer to 6.

- I live in moist forests as well as in meadows and other open areas.

- I am most active in the mornings and after rain.

- I rarely travel far away from home and may spend my entire life in little more than one acre.

- I can live to be more than 100 years old!

- Females of my species can store sperm after mating and lay fertile eggs for several years.

- I eat many kinds of food, including berries, grass, earthworms, mushrooms, snails, slugs, and insects.

- When young, we are often eaten by crows. People sometimes eat us, but many have died because of the toxins in our flesh from eating poisonous mushrooms.

- I am usually brown but am often covered with numerous yellow and orange stripes and spots.

- My eyes are either red or brown in color, depending on my sex.

EASTERN BOX TURTLE

What animal am I?

- I weigh 5 to 14 pounds when fully grown.

- I am most active during the daytime.

- I like to eat soft, succulent plants, such as clover, plantain, grass, and alfalfa, as well as corn and other garden plants.

- I live as far north as Alaska and as far south as Alabama.

- When I'm angry or alarmed, I whistle, hiss, squeal, or growl.

- I hibernate in the winter on a bed of grass in a special underground chamber.

- When I am hibernating, I only breathe once every six minutes and my heart only beats 4 times a minute.

- I am a good swimmer and I can climb trees.

- I live alone (except for when I have babies) in a deep burrow, up to five feet deep and 30 feet long, with two or more entrances.

- There is a special chamber in my burrow where I go to the bathroom.

GROUNDHOG (WOODCHUCK)

What animal am I?

- I usually live near shallow water in cone-shaped houses up to five feet tall that are made of vegetation and have one or more underwater entrances.

- I weigh about 2 to 4 pounds when full grown and my tail is almost as long as my body.

- I am an excellent swimmer with webbed hind feet. I spend lots of time in the water and can even swim backwards!

- Water plants, such as cattails and waterlilies, fish, frogs, crayfish, mussels, and clams are my favorite food items.

- I have two or three litters a year with as few as one and as many as nine babies in each litter.

- If my babies are threatened by high water, I will carry them one by one to safety in my mouth.

- People trap me for my meat and fur.

- Though I am originally from North America, I have become common in Europe and parts of Asia.

- My enemies are owls, foxes, large predatory fish, snapping turtles, minks, raccoons, otters, and people.

- I am named for the scent that I produce with special glands in my groin area.

MUSKRAT

What animal am I?

- I spend most of my time in the forest, or in nearby swamps, fields, and brushy areas.

- I am most active during the night.

- I am usually reddish in the summer and bluish-gray in the winter.

- I eat up to nine pounds of food a day, including acorns, nuts, corn, and the twigs and buds of woody plants. These include maples, birches, viburnums, and pines and other conifers.

- My stomach is divided into four parts and I can digest food that other animals cannot.

- We spend the summers in small groups, but as many as 150 of us may join together in the winter. These groups are led by a mature female.

- I can run up to 40 miles per hour and I can jump more than 8 feet high and 30 feet across.

- I can live more than 16 years in the wild.

- I am usually weaned before I am 3 months old, but stay with my mother for about a year, or sometimes two years.

- I can weigh up to 400 pounds, though I usually weigh closer to 200 pounds.

- Over six million of my kind are killed by hunters in the United States each year.

WHITE-TAILED DEER (stag with fawn)

What animal am I?

- I eat a variety of seeds and nuts and plant bulbs, as well as insects, slugs, snails, birds' eggs, and dead animals.

- When I run, I hold my tail straight up in the air.

- We live alone except for mothers and babies.

- I hibernate during the winter, but I wake up every two weeks or so to get something to eat.

- My burrows are up to 10 feet long and have chambers for my leaf-lined nest and for food storage.

- I am a chatterbox and make a variety of noises, including "chucks", "chips" and "chirps."

- I live in the forest and in brushy areas and I often live near people or in cemeteries.

- I weigh five ounces or less when I am full-grown.

- My main predators are long-tailed weasels, hawks, foxes, bobcats, and house cats.

- I can fit up to eight acorns in my cheeks at one time!

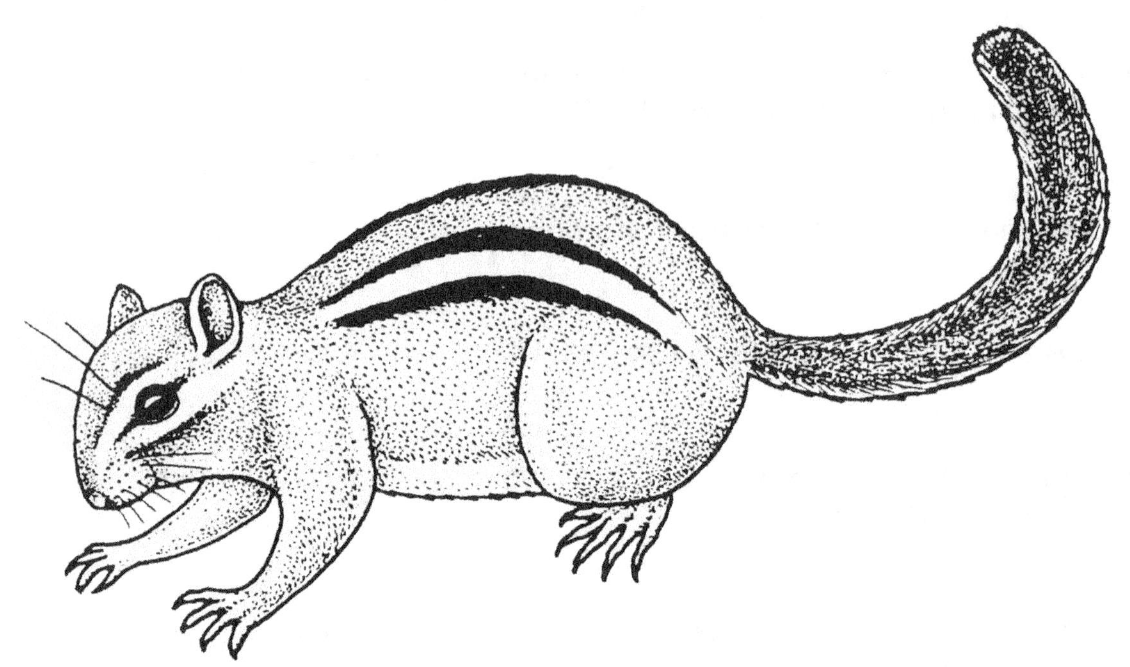

EASTERN CHIPMUNK

What animal am I?

- I am mostly black in color, but my face is brown and I often have a patch of white fur on my breast.

- My mouth contains 42 teeth.

- I have six nipples, but usually only have two babies at a time.

- My babies are born in the winter.

- I will eat almost anything, including garbage, but most of my food is vegetation.

- I can run 30 miles an hour for short distances.

- Night is my most active time of day.

- I am a good swimmer and climber of trees.

- I often live to be 30 years old.

- My home range can be from 8 to 25 square miles in size.

- I may be found from northern Alaska and Canada to Florida.

- I can grow up to six feet long and almost 600 pounds, but I only weigh about seven ounces when I am born.

BLACK BEAR

What animal am I?

- I live in trees and eat deciduous leaves, such as cherry, oak, apple, and maple.

- I am usually about two inches long.

- The lower part of my long hind legs is covered with short, sharp spines.

- I have wings, but only when fully mature.

- I have ears on my front legs!

- We are eaten by many creatures, including lizards, praying mantises, tree frogs, birds, and mammals including bats.

- I lay my eggs in tree bark crevices or on stems in the fall. They hatch in the spring.

- I am bright green in color and blend in well with my background.

- We are vocal at night when mature, repeating a three or four syllable song over and over again.

TRUE KATYDID

What animal am I?

- I live on the bottom in shallow salt water in the summer, burrowing into the sand or mud.

- In the winter, I move offshore into water that is 150 to 200 feet deep.

- I can change color to blend in with my surroundings.

- I have numerous dark spots on my body.

- I am most active during the day.

- I eat many kinds of fish, including menhaden, young bluefish, porgies, and even smaller members of my own kind.

- I also eat crabs, mollusks, and shrimp.

- I can live to be 20 years old.

- I can grow to weigh as much as 26 pounds, with females usually being larger than males.

- After I am born, my body changes and one of my eyes gradually moves from one side of my head to the other.

SUMMER FLOUNDER

What animal am I?

- I am about 21 inches wide, 12 inches long, and weigh up to about 6 ounces when grown.

- I often live on farms, in towns, and even in big cities.

- I lay 4 to 5 white eggs with brown spots – but I don't build a nest for them. Instead I use natural or manmade cavities, or abandoned nests.

- Females of my kind do most of the egg-sitting.

- Males feed the females while they are egg-sitting and bring most of the food to the babies after they have hatched.

- Small birds, insects, lizards, and rodents are my favorite foods.

- I have bold coloring with areas of reddish brown, white, blue gray (on males), black, tan, and I have dark spots and bars over most of my body.

- I usually look for food from the top of a pole or tree, but capture it on the ground rather than in the air.

- I can hover in the air.

- I can be trained by humans to hunt small game for them.

- My high-pitched, rapid, piercing call sounds like *klee klee klee klee klee klee.*

AMERICAN KESTREL

What animal am I?

- I can grow to be 40 inches long, 7 ½ feet wide, and weigh as much as 14 pounds.

- I like to live near water – lakes, marshes, rivers, bays, or the ocean.

- My favorite food is fish, which I catch by snatching them from the water with my feet. I will also eat dead fish when I find them.

- I also sometimes eat water birds as large as geese and rodents, rabbits, raccoons, seals, and even deer fawns.

- Sometimes I steal food from other animals.

- I lay one to four white eggs in nests that I make out of twigs and branches high up in trees or on the top of rocky cliffs.

- I use the same nests year after year, making repairs as needed. A single nest may weigh as much as 2,000 pounds!

- I can fly at over 40 miles per hour, but my diving speed may be almost 100 miles per hour!

- My range extends from northern Mexico and Florida to northern Canada and Alaska.

- My lifespan in the wild is usually around 20-30 years, but I have lived to be almost 50 years old in captivity.

- I am mostly dark brown to almost black in color, with large patches of white and a yellow bill.

Answer on NEXT PAGE

BALD EAGLE

What animal am I?

- Our females guard their clutches of up to 17 eggs. They may not eat any food until their eggs have hatched after six to eight weeks!

- We live under rocks and logs in moist places, usually in wooded areas.

- I can grow up to five inches long, but am less than an inch long at birth, most of that being my tail. I look like a miniature adult at birth.

- We form mated pairs when we are sexually mature at five years of age.

- I don't have any lungs. Instead, I breathe through my skin, but it must remain moist for me to breathe.

- I can live to be 25 years old.

- I eat small invertebrates, such as termites, snails, worms, centipedes, and pill bugs.

- I can regrow many of my body parts if they are lost through injury, including legs, tails, and even portions of my head.

- My enemies include snakes, salamanders, toads, and spiders.

- My skin is shiny and moist, with no hairs, feathers, or scales. It has a bacterium on it that protects me from fungus.

- I have a long reddish stripe running down the length of my body, though this stripe is gray in some of my kind.

RED-BACKED SALAMANDER

What animal am I?

- I live on the seacoasts and near lakes.

- I am up to 12 feet wide, six feet long, and weigh up to 30 pounds.

- I form large breeding colonies consisting of as many as 5,000 mated pairs.

- Males of my species grow a flat keel on top of our bills during the breeding season.

- When I fly, I alternate flapping and gliding and rise to great heights above the land.

- I am all white except for patches of black on my wingtips and some gray on the back of my head.

- Besides fish, I also eat crayfish and salamanders.

- I scoop up fish with my very large bill while wading in shallow water. I do not dive into the water in search of food.

- We cooperate when feeding, forming a line and flapping our wings to drive fish into shallower water.

- I live 15 to 25 years in the wild.

- My main predators are sea gulls, great horned owls, red-tailed hawks, ravens, eagles, red foxes, and coyotes – but only the last of these will attack me when I am full-grown.

WHITE PELICAN

What animal am I?

- I usually don't live more than three years, but I can have babies when I am only six weeks old.

- In warm climates, I can have 8 litters a year!

- I can have as many as 16 babies at a time, but seven is average.

- I am descended from Iranian ancestors, who came to North America via Europe.

- I may spend the summer in fields, but move into human dwellings for the winter.

- We live in groups and like to groom each other.

- I eat almost anything that is edible, including leather, soap, and glue.

- I am a good singer and sound something like a canary.

- Albino members of my species are commonly studied in laboratories.

- I weigh less than one ounce!

- I like to live near people, but most people don't like to live near me.

HOUSE MOUSE

What animal am I?

- Sometimes I nest in colonies; sometimes I nest alone. I build a nest of sticks lined with soft bedding, either in a tree or on the ground.

- My voice is a low croak.

- I fly with my long neck folded into an "S" shape.

- I live near water – either fresh, salt, or brackish.

- I am mostly grayish blue, with small patches of white, black, tan, and reddish brown. However, some of us who live in Florida are all white.

- Adult males of my kind have long dark crests.

- We range from Alaska to Mexico to the West Indies. We have even been known to breed in the Galapagos Islands in the Pacific Ocean.

- I can be over four feet long and six feet wide, but I only weigh a maximum of around eight pounds.

- I eat mostly fish, but will also eat mice, frogs, small mammals, birds, reptiles, and crustaceans. I hunt for food while wading or standing still in shallow water.

- Most of us migrate south in the winter, but a few of us don't bother.

GREAT BLUE HERON

What animal am I?

- When grown, I am usually between three and five feet long.

- I mature very slowly and am not fully mature until I am 11 years old (males) or as much as 21 years old (females). I can live to be 100 years old.

- I am migratory and have been known to travel 5,000 miles from Washington State to Japan.

- I am grayish brown in color, but lighter on my underside.

- I mate in the winter and have litters of two to eleven young.

- My offspring are born live after a gestation period of up to two years. This is perhaps the longest gestation period of any known animal.

- I live in ocean waters up to 2,000 feet deep or more, but am usually found in shallow waters.

- I am mostly a bottom dweller and eat fish up to three times my size. I also eat squid and jellyfish. We often hunt in packs.

- I live along the coasts of every continent except for Antarctica.

- I have sharp spines with venom glands on my back that can inject poison into an attacker.

Answer on NEXT PAGE

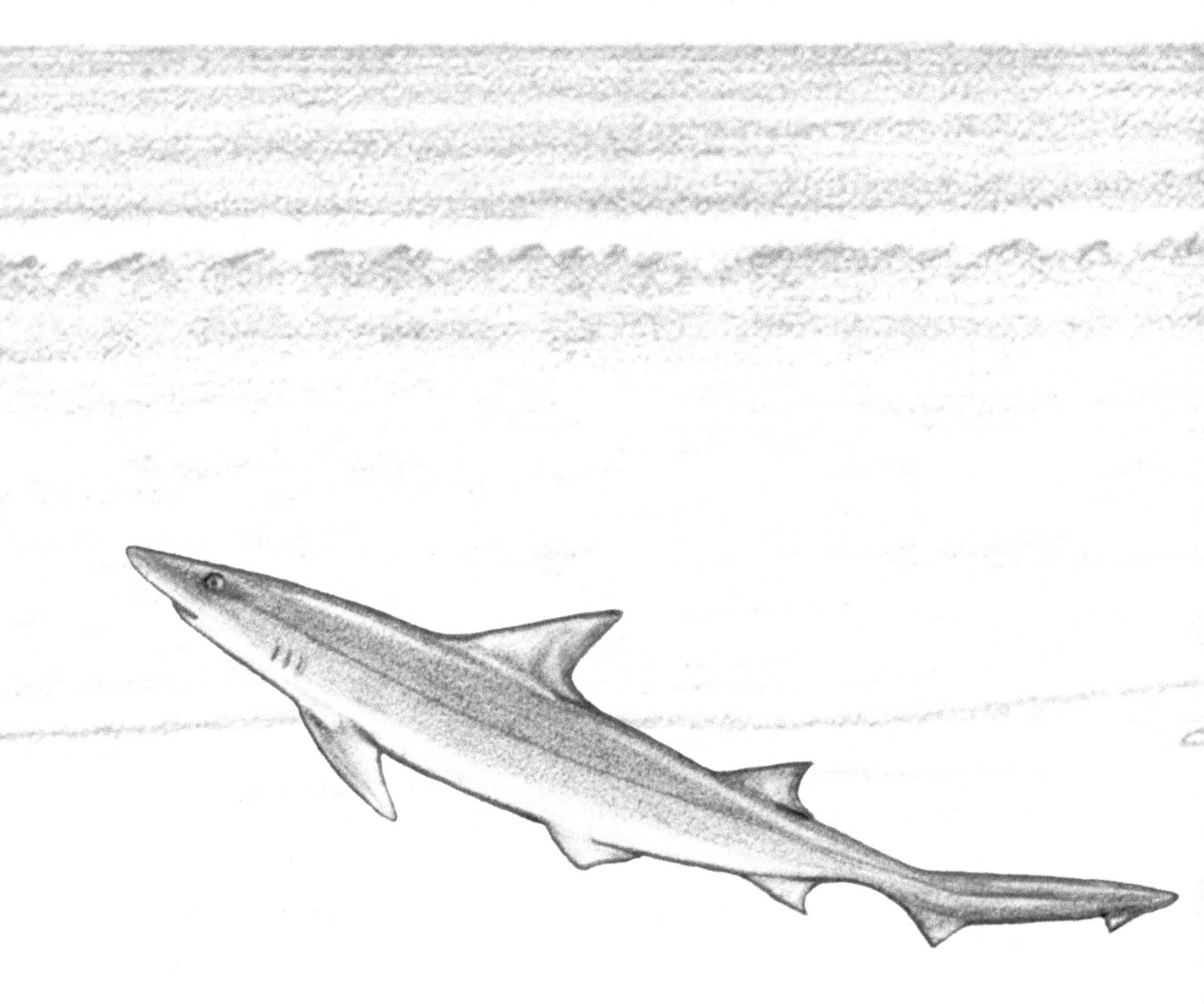

SPINY DOGFISH SHARK

What animal am I?

- I live in temperate waters throughout the world – except in the eastern Pacific Ocean.

- I live in large groups of individuals that are all about the same age.

- My teeth are extremely sharp and I use them to eat many kinds of fish.

- I also eat squid, crabs, and shrimp.

- When we are attacking schools of fish, they will sometimes jump onto the beach in large numbers to escape from us.

- I have been known to attack people when feeding.

- I look for food anywhere in the water column, from the bottom to the surface.

- I can weigh up to 30 or even 40 pounds, but 20 pounds and three feet in length is my normal size when full-grown.

- My life span is about 9 to 12 years.

- My main predators are sharks, tuna, swordfish, and humans.

- I am migratory and travel hundreds of miles along the coasts, following schools of fish.

- I am bluish green on top and silver underneath, with a sharply forked tail and a dark spot at the base of my pectoral fin.

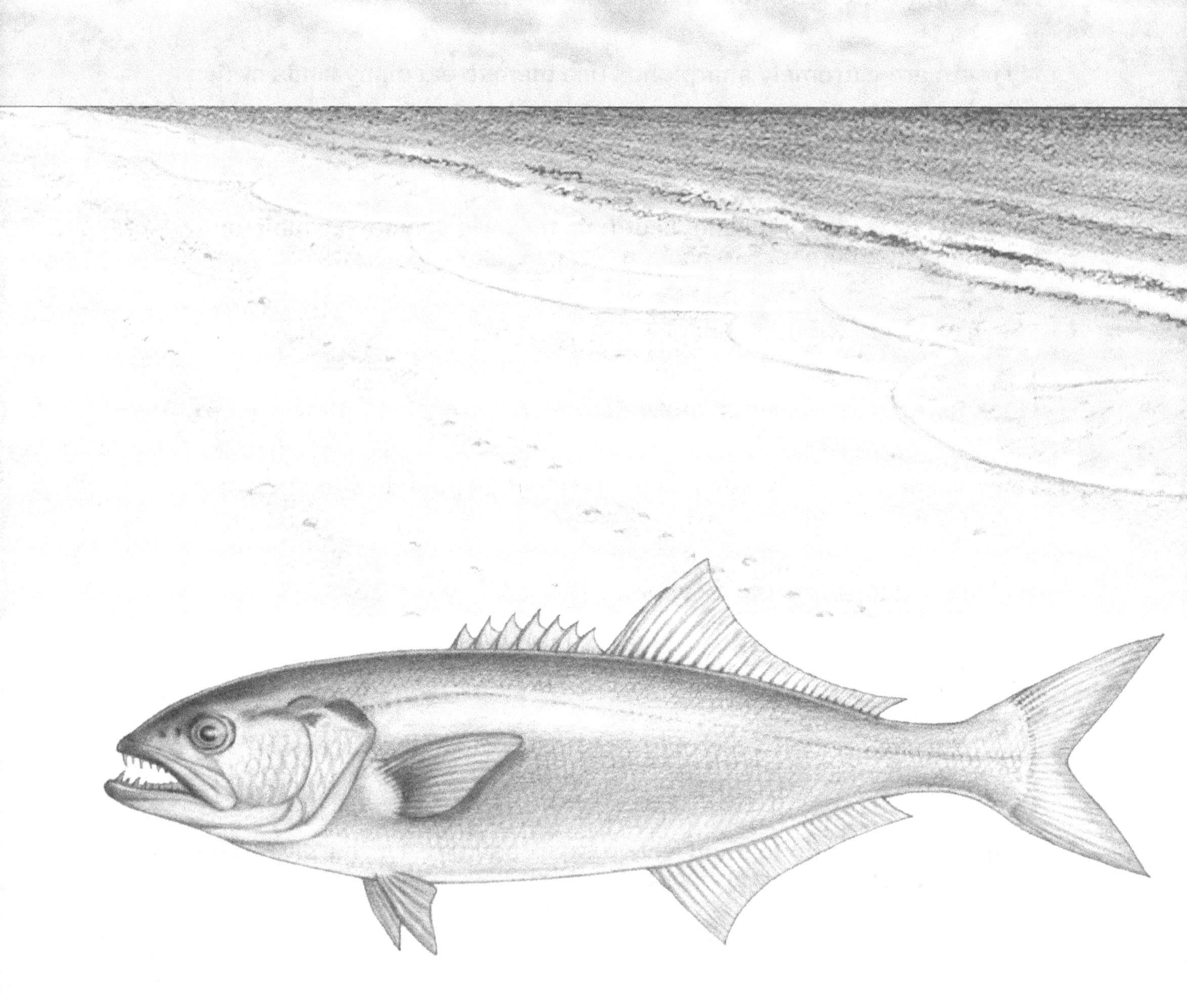

BLUEFISH

What animal am I?

- When full-grown, I weigh less than half an ounce, but I am 12 inches wide.

- I eat insects, especially moths, but also mosquitoes, beetles, and flies.

- I have two nipples and only have one baby at a time.

- I hibernate in the winter.

- I am active at night and sleep during the day.

- I can roll my ears up on the sides of my head.

- I live at least 10 years – and maybe as long as 30 years.

- I can hover like a hummingbird.

- I can find my way around in total darkness.

- I live in buildings, caves, tunnels, hollow trees, and under bridges.

EASTERN BIG-EARED BAT

What animal am I?

- It has been estimated that there were one billion of my kind before the European settlers arrived in North America.

- I weigh about a pound to a pound and a half when full-grown.

- I live in hardwood forests and near rivers, but I don't mind living in town if there are trees.

- I have two kinds of home: leaf nests in tree branches and dens in tree cavities. I also make above-ground resting platforms out of leaves.

- I use my tail as an umbrella, blanket, sunshade, and even as a rudder when I go swimming.

- I am most active in the morning and in the evening.

- I usually have two litters of two or three babies each per year.

- Flower buds, mushrooms, seeds, nuts, tree bark, fruits, corn, and acorns are my favorite foods – not necessarily in that order.

- I'm about the size of a loaf of bread, but I can run 20 miles an hour – as fast as most professional athletes.

- If taken far away from where I live, I am good at finding my way home.

- I am usually gray with some white and reddish markings, but may also be all black or even all white.

EASTERN GRAY SQUIRREL

What animal am I?

- I have 42 teeth – ten more than a human being.

- I'm most active at night and like to keep to myself.

- I make my home under boulders, in hollow logs, or in underground burrows.

- I'm not a very fussy eater. I like rabbits, mice, voles, squirrels, insects, shellfish, lizards, fruits, acorns, berries, persimmons, grasshoppers, grass, turkeys, chickens, and eggs.

- I can run 28 miles per hour, which is a little bit faster than the fastest human.

- The male of my species helps feed and care for its young, but lives apart.

- I'm ready to hunt for myself when I am four months old.

- My enemies are bobcats, eagles, wolves, coyotes, dogs, and people.

- I am an excellent tree climber.

- I'm about three feet long and weigh up to 13 pounds – usually closer to 10 pounds.

GRAY FOX

What animal am I?

- My most active times of day are the morning and evening.

- I live in large groups made up of both sexes in the winter, but we split into groups of males or females only in the summer.

- I eat grass, tree bark, lichen, twigs, and herbs.

- I can live to be 25 years old.

- In the springtime, I often move up into the mountains, then return to lower country in the fall.

- My call is a high-pitched squeal or whistle or series of grunts.

- I can walk just a few minutes after I am born.

- The largest of my kind can run up to 35 miles per hour.

- An alpha male of my species may have as many as 60 mates.

- My main predators are mountain lions, bears, and people.

- I can weigh more than 1,000 pounds!

ELK (WAPITI)

What animal am I?

- I have excellent senses of smell and hearing, but my eyesight is not very good.

- I can run up to 30 miles per hour – faster than the fastest human.

- I come in a variety of colors, including brown, yellowish, gray, and black.

- We are usually born as a pair of twins.

- I am most active at night.

- We often dig our own dens and return to them winter after winter.

- I don't actually hibernate and can easily be awakened during a winter sleep.

- I eat a wide variety of foods, including nuts, berries, fish, insects, small mammals, grass, sheep, goats, nuts, roots, and many other things.

- In the wild, I may live more than 30 years, but one of us once lived to be 47 in captivity!

- I can weigh more than 1,000 pounds!

GRIZZLY BEAR

What animal am I?

- I am boldly colored with areas of reddish tan, white, and black.

- I am the fastest land animal in North America and can run up to 70 miles an hour!

- I shed my large black horns every year and grow new ones.

- Though my second name suggests that I am related to a common type of animal, I am actually one of a kind, with no close relatives.

- In winter we form large herds of both sexes and all ages.

- I eat weeds, cacti, grass, and sagebrush.

- I have the same number of teeth as human beings – 32.

- I have excellent eyesight and can detect movements four miles away!

- I am most active during the day, but stay awake most of the night.

- I weigh between 75 and 140 pounds when full-grown.

- My main enemies are coyotes, wolves, and humans.

PRONGHORN ANTELOPE

What animal am I?

- When fully grown, I can weigh as much as 300 pounds.

- I live in rugged areas in the western part of North America, such as the slopes of mountains and in deserts.

- My predators are wolves, mountain lions, bears, golden eagles (when I am young), coyotes, bobcats, lynxes, and humans.

- We live in large groups, with both sexes together in the winter but mature males living separately in the summer.

- We only have one baby at a time, born in late spring or early summer.

- I eat grasses and sedges and woody plants like sagebrush and willows. I also eat small flowering plants, such as clover and phlox, and cacti in the desert.

- I am active during the day and rest at night, unless having too many people around forces me to eat during the night.

- My hooves are hard on the outside and spongy in the center, which enables me to climb steep rock cliffs.

- In the fall, males do battle to establish who can mate. We charge each other at more than 20 miles per hour, colliding headfirst.

- The sound of our heads banging together is so loud it can be heard a mile away!

BIG-HORN SHEEP

What animal am I?

- I live in tropical seas all over the world and spend a lot of time near coral reefs.

- I am usually 3 feet long and weigh 180 pounds when full-grown. However, I have been known to weigh as much as 280 pounds.

- I weigh less than one ounce when I am born.

- I am old enough to breed when I am 2 to 4 years old, but I am not fully mature until I am at least 10 to 25 years old.

- I eat mostly sponges, but will also take fish, anemones, crustaceans, and algae.

- I can actually glow in the dark!

- I am a wonderful swimmer and look like I am flying underwater.

- I often rest in underwater caves and on ledges.

- I breathe air and have to come to the surface every so often.

- My enemies include sharks, humans, crocodiles, and large fish.

- When I am young, I am often eaten by sea gulls and other shore birds, crabs, and many kinds of fish.

- I make my nests on beaches in many parts of the world and usually lay about 140 eggs in the sand.

HAWKSBILL TURTLE

What animal am I?

- I can weigh up to 35 pounds.

- I live in a variety of habitats, including forests, swamps, and chaparral.

- I am an excellent tree climber.

- I may live as long as 25 years.

- I am most active at night.

- My den is usually underground, in rock crevices, or in a hollow log.

- I usually live alone, unless I have babies with me.

- My favorite foods are birds, reptiles, and mammals, including raccoons, opossums, rabbits, hares, squirrels, deer, and even skunks, but I will eat carrion if it is fresh.

- I can go a long time without food, but when I eat, I can eat a lot at one time.

- I have dark spots over most of my body.

- I have a very short tail.

BOBCAT

What animal am I?

- I have dark spots when I am very young, but they disappear as I grow older.

- I can grow to 9 feet long and weigh up to 275 pounds.

- I am the most widely distributed American mammal and can be found from northern Canada to southern South America.

- I can be found in high mountains, steaming jungles, and dry deserts.

- I mate at any time of year and my young can be born in any month. When mating, we will hunt together and sleep side by side.

- I can be active during the day or night, but I am usually nocturnal where people are common.

- My long tail is dark at its tip.

- I mostly eat deer, but will also take hares, beavers, porcupines, ground hogs, raccoons, coyotes, birds, and even grasshoppers.

- I can range widely in search of food, traveling as far as 25 miles in one night!

- I can run faster than a deer for short distances.

- I sometimes eat domesticated animals, like sheep and cattle – and even horses!

Answer on NEXT PAGE

MOUNTAIN LION (COUGAR)

What animal am I?

- I am about an inch long when grown.

- My body is black with yellow bands and zigzags. My legs are reddish brown.

- I have long antennae that are two thirds as long as my body if I am a male and one half as long if I am a female.

- I am born in the fall and burrow in Black Locust trees.

- The tunnels that I make in locust trees are only about 4 inches long and a quarter inch wide, but they may allow damaging fungi to enter the wood.

- When I am one year old, I leave my burrow and fly away.

- As an adult, I eat pollen and nectar on goldenrod flowers.

- After mating, I lay my eggs on the bark of a Black Locust tree.

- From a distance, I am often mistaken for a yellow jacket or wasp, but I cannot sting.

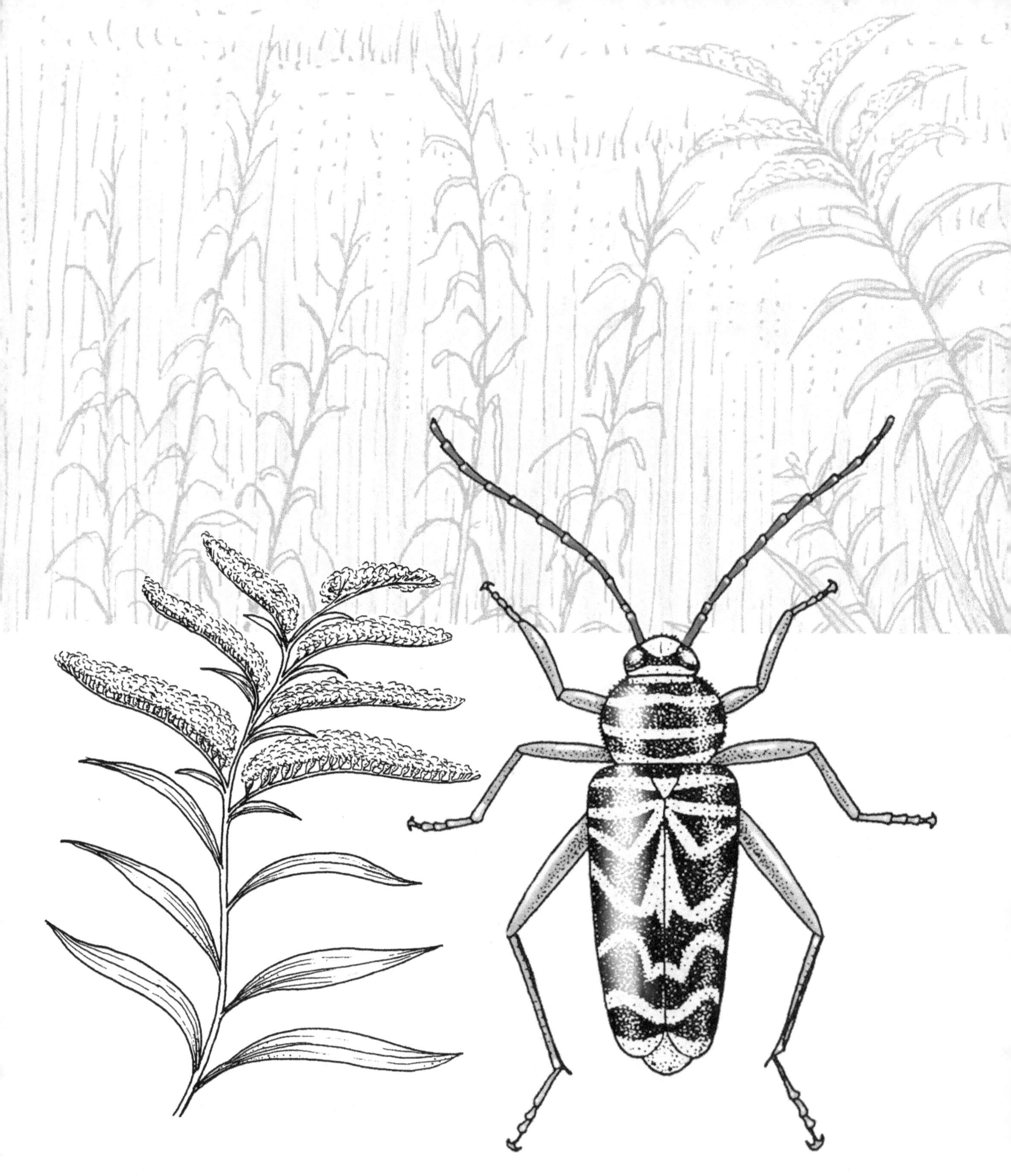

LOCUST BORER BEETLE (with Golden Rod)

What animal am I?

- I live near streams, rivers, ponds, and lakes.

- I eat crabs, fish, frogs, snakes, crayfish, clams, and other aquatic creatures. I also eat mice and insects.

- I am a marvelous swimmer, with webbed feet and tiny ears.

- I can swim underwater for a quarter of a mile without ever surfacing for air.

- I am usually active during the day.

- I create places where I can slide on the ice or snow or mud into the water over and over again, just for fun.

- Until I am three months old, my mother keeps my father away, but then she lets him join the family and teach me how to hunt and play.

- I can weigh up to 30 pounds when full-grown.

- When pursuing fish for food, we will often work together.

- I make my den in the bank of a stream or lake, with underwater and aboveground entrances.

- I make a wide variety of sounds, including whistles, chirps, chuckles, snorts, and growls.

RIVER OTTER

What animal am I?

- I eat fruits, berries, nuts, and grains as well as crabs, snails, crayfish, frogs, insects, mice, squirrels, rats, baby muskrats, birds, turtles, eggs, honey, and peoples' garbage.

- I often dip my food in water before eating it.

- I can weigh up to 48 pounds, but am usually closer to 25 pounds when full-grown.

- I weigh only two ounces when I am born.

- I am very vocal and make a wide variety of sounds.

- I like to live in wooded areas near water, but I also live in towns and cities.

- I have a long, bushy, ringed tail.

- I am an excellent climber – I can even come down a tree trunk headfirst!

- I am most active at night.

- I don't hibernate in the winter, but may take very long naps, sometimes sleeping for a month or more at one time.

- My hands are very nimble – I can even turn doorknobs.

- My main enemies are coyotes, bobcats, owls, foxes, and people.

RACCOON

What animal am I?

- I build sturdy nests that are lined with mud and reinforced with twigs and string for my 3-5 blue-green eggs.

- I can raise up to three broods per year.

- I eat earthworms, insects, seeds, and berries.

- My range extends from Alaska to Guatemala.

- My voice is musical and I sometimes sound like I am saying *cheerup-cheerily-cheerup-cheerily.*

- When I am running, I often stop suddenly and stand perfectly still, then start running again.

- I often live in towns, cities, and farm land and like to search for food in peoples' yards.

- I usually retreat to moist northern woodlands and swamps for the winter and join large flocks in the late winter to early spring.

- It is estimated that 80 per cent of us die each winter.

- When grown, I am reddish and dark gray to almost black, with a few small areas of white, and am about ten inches long.

ROBIN

What animal am I?

- I am one of the most common mammals east of the Mississippi River.

- I can grow to five inches in length and one ounce in weight.

- I eat fungi, earthworms, centipedes, beetles, snails, insects, mice – and even my own kind.

- I eat at least half and sometimes more than my own weight in food every day.

- I live mostly underground in tunnels and in nests under rocks, logs, or other debris.

- I have no external ears and my eyes are so small you can hardly see them.

- I have a very flexible, very sensitive nose that helps me find food.

- When first born, I am about the size of a honeybee.

- I only live two years at the most.

- I have a poisonous bite that paralyzes my prey.

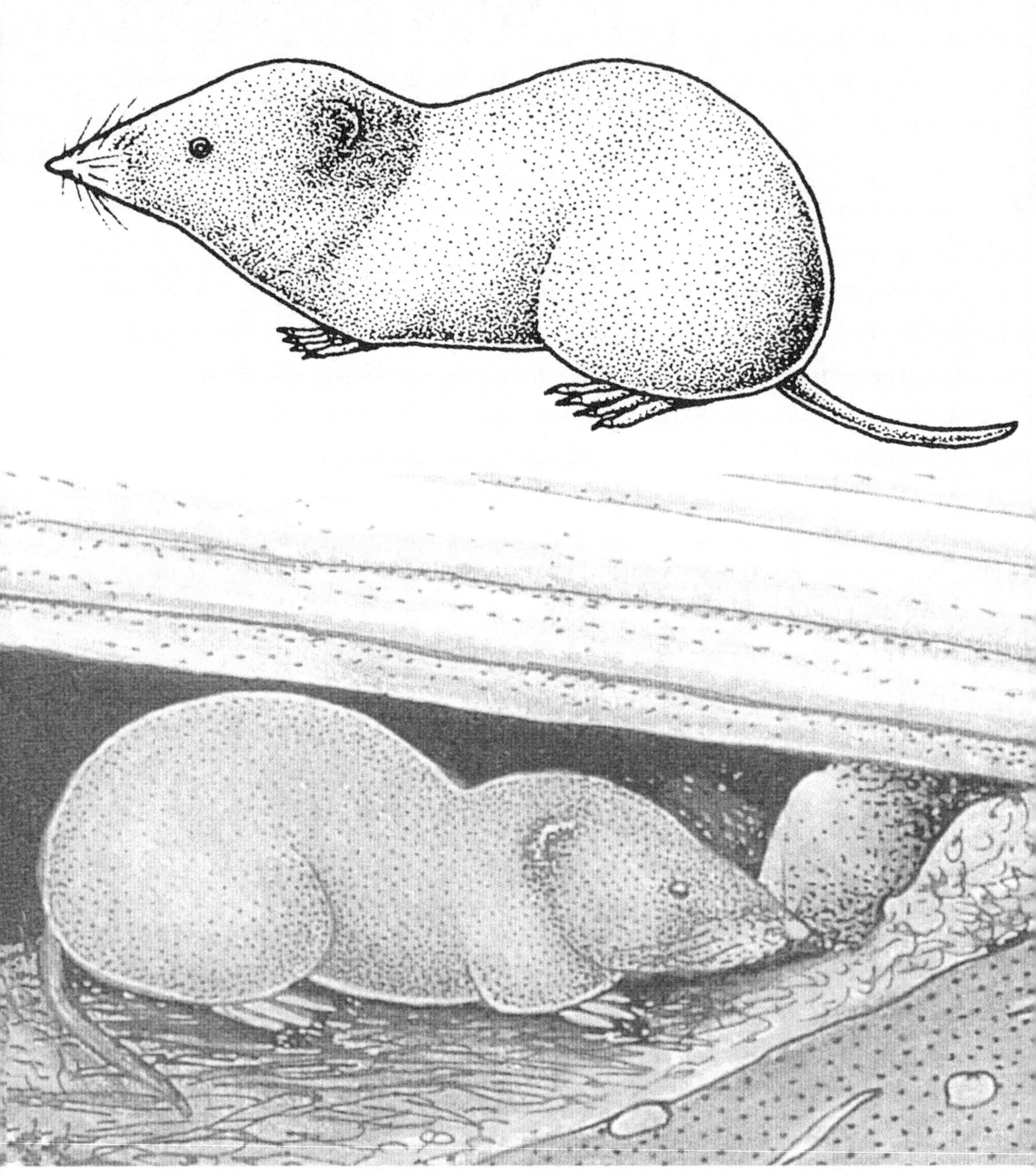

NORTHERN SHORT-TAILED SHREW

What animal am I?

- When I am born, I am hairless and helpless and weigh only one twentieth of an ounce.

- I am ready to leave my mother and live on my own when I am only three weeks old.

- I eat earthworms, crustaceans, insects, and fish.

- I have 44 teeth.

- I like to live in moist areas near swamps, lakes, or streams.

- Though I live in the northeastern United States and Canada, I do not hibernate.

- My senses of smell and sight are weak.

- I dig in snow as readily as in soil.

- My burrows open into streams, lakes, or ponds.

- I am an excellent swimmer.

- My nose is divided into 22 movable tentacles which are extremely sensitive and help me find prey.

STAR-NOSED MOLE

What animal am I?

- I build very large nests of sticks and branches in trees, on rocks, or on level ground near water and reuse them year after year.

- I lay two to four white or buff-colored, brown-spotted eggs.

- I always live near water, along coastlines, rivers, and lakes.

- My voice consists of repeated loud chirps and cheeps.

- I grow up to two feet long and six feet wide and may weigh almost five pounds.

- Almost all of my food consists of fish. Rarely, I will eat small birds, rodents, rabbits, hares, and small reptiles.

- I am good at hovering while looking for food, then plunge feet-first into the water to grasp my prey.

- I can close my nostrils when underwater.

- I am mostly white underneath and mostly brown on top.

- My range is vast – from Argentina to Alaska as well as Europe, Asia, Australia, and Africa. However, I am not very common.

OSPREY

What animal am I?

- I like to live in moist forests near lakes and swamps.

- I often live 20 years or more.

- I weigh as much as 35 pounds when I am born.

- I am most active during the night.

- In winter, I eat mostly twigs, bark, and saplings; in summer, I eat mostly willows and aquatic plants like water lilies.

- I am a fast swimmer (six miles per hour) and can run up to 35 miles per hour on land.

- I may cover myself in mud or submerge myself completely in water to avoid flies and mosquitoes.

- I am solitary in the summer, but live in small groups during the winter.

- Wolves and humans are my main predators.

- During the mating season, males may charge each other, people, cars, and even trains!

- I can be up to 7 ½ feet tall and weigh as much as 1800 pounds!

MOOSE

What animal am I?

- I live in the forests of eastern North America.

- When I am young, I eat the leaves of trees, including oaks, persimmons, hickories, walnuts, birches, and sweet gums.

- As an adult, I have purplish wing margins when I appear in the spring, but yellow wing margins when I appear in the summer.

- As an adult, I am usually around 4 ½ inches wide, though 7 inch giants have been seen.

- I am most active at night as an adult.

- Adults of my kind never eat and don't even have mouths! We only live for a few days – just long enough to mate and lay eggs.

- Females may lay as many as 600 eggs, depositing just a few at a time on the underside of leaves.

- My hind wings have tail-like structures at the bottom that can be expanded in size and are useful in fooling bats that try to eat me on the wing.

- My wings are pale green in color and my body is white and covered with hairs.

- I have four eyespots on my wings to scare away predators.

LUNA MOTH

What animal am I?

- I live in white pine forests and suck the juices from the tender tips of white pine twigs.

- A sweet sticky substance drops from my rear end onto whatever is beneath me.

- I am black with numerous white markings on my sides and down the middle of my back.

- I live with so many of my kind that we may almost completely cover pine twigs and small branches.

- Females can reproduce without having mated and without laying eggs.

- When I am first born, I look just like an adult, only smaller.

- When cold weather approaches, special winged offspring of both sexes are produced, which mate with each other.

- After mating, the winged females lay rows of shiny black eggs, which are glued in single file to the edges of white pine needles.

- Only our eggs survive the winter.

WHITE PINE APHID (with White Pine twig)

What animal am I?

- I usually live in the forest.

- I eat acorns, cherry pits, berries, seeds, beetles, caterpillars, flower buds – and even others of my own kind!

- I line my nests with a variety of materials, including feathers, grass, moss, hair, and bits of cloth.

- I am an excellent climber and often climb trees, using my tail for balance.

- I have two to four litters per year and can have babies when I am only 10 weeks old.

- I can live to be five years old.

- When I am alarmed, I often drum my front feet rapidly.

- My main predators are snakes, birds, and many kinds of mammals.

- I can be brown, reddish brown, or gray, with a white underside.

- When full-grown, I weigh about one ounce and am about four inches long, not including my long tail.

- My ears are one inch long.

WHITE-FOOTED MOUSE

What animal am I?

- I am about five or six inches long when grown.

- I like to live near people and usually build my nests in man-made structures.

- I weave my nests from pieces of grass, string, straw, twigs, feathers, and bits of paper and use them all year round.

- Males occasionally sit on our clutches of 3 to 7 speckled white eggs.

- I usually have two or three broods per season.

- Even though my eggs are only laid one per day, they all hatch at the same time.

- The first of my kind in North America were brought from England in 1850.

- My song is a monotonous chorus of shrill cheeps, repeated over and over.

- My food consists of weed seeds, grains like corn, wheat, and oats, and insects during the warmer months.

- I will even eat dead insects that collect on the fronts of cars and trucks.

HOUSE SPARROW (female left, male right)

What animal am I?

- My food includes grass, rice, seeds, aquatic plants, snails, crabs, insects, bird eggs, and young birds.

- When full-grown, I can weigh almost three ounces and be a foot long.

- I only have 16 teeth – half as many as a human.

- I like to live in marshy areas.

- I am at home in the water and am an excellent diver and swimmer.

- I am most active at night.

- I am sexually mature when I am 50 days old and may have several litters a year.

- I can breed at any time of the year.

- My tail is mostly hairless.

- My main predators are hawks, barn owls, and snakes such as water moccasins.

MARSH RICE RAT

What animal am I?

- I am a fast swimmer, but fairly slow-moving on land.

- I can walk on my hind legs.

- I can float in water with only my eyes and nose showing.

- I live in swampy, marshy places near water.

- I eat reeds, greenbrier, tree leaves and twigs, amaryllis, plant bulbs, and wild potatoes.

- I weigh about three pounds and grow up to 17 inches long.

- My ears are much longer than my tail.

- I am dark brown with a grayish underside.

- I am most active at night.

- Great horned owls, hawks, and people are among my predators.

MARSH RABBIT

What animal am I?

- Some of my favorite foods are fruits, berries, insects, earthworms, spiders, snails, snakes, amphibians, birds, eggs, and mice.

- I like to live on prairies, brushy areas, and in forests with some open areas, but I don't mind living close to town.

- I am most active during the night and I do not hibernate in the winter.

- Coyotes, mountain lions, and minks will eat me, but only if they are very hungry.

- Great horned owls also eat me, and without hesitation.

- I have 10 to 14 nipples.

- I have as many as 10 babies at a time, but usually only 5 or 6.

- I live in underground burrows with as many as five well-hidden entrances.

- I weigh up to 14 pounds and may grow up to 31 inches long, almost half of which is a bushy tail.

- When I encounter an enemy, I raise my tail, clash my teeth, and drum on the ground with my forefeet. And that's not all I can do!

- I am black and white.

STRIPED SKUNK

What animal am I?

- I usually live in rocky, wooded areas.

- I am active during the day in the spring and fall; at night during the summer.

- I may be yellowish, brownish, grayish, or almost black in color, with dark cross bands across my body.

- My favorite food is rodents, such as chipmunks, squirrels, and mice. I also eat small birds.

- My principal enemies are king snakes, birds of prey, and human beings.

- I give birth to between 5 and 17 live young about one foot long. I can grow to be over six feet long.

- I am usually solitary, but often spend the winter hibernating in dens with many others of my kind as well as other species.

- Males of my kind may have wrestling matches to determine who gets to mate.

- I can live to be over 30 years old.

- I have no voice but can make a loud, alarming noise.

TIMBER RATTLESNAKE

What animal am I?

- I am yellowish red when born, but gradually turn dark brown.

- I often plaster myself with mud to ward off insects.

- I can live to be more than 30 years old.

- I have a long tail with a tuft of fur at the end of it.

- I am most active during the day – especially morning and afternoon – but also at night when the moon is bright.

- I mostly eat grasses, but also sedges, berries, horsetails, small flowering plants, and lichens.

- I am a good swimmer and can run up to 32 miles per hour.

- I usually live in plains and on prairies, but occasionally in forests.

- Normally, I am pregnant for nine months and give birth to one infant – just like humans.

- I like to live with others of my kind and we form very large groups during the summer breeding season.

- I can be over six feet tall and weigh over 2,000 pounds, making me the largest land animal in North America!

BISON (BUFFALO)

What animal am I?

- I build my nest in the woods with branches and twigs lined with grass, shredded bark, and dead leaves, but I feed in open country.

- Besides forests, I live in deserts, farmlands, and grasslands and even in towns and cities.

- I am usually about four feet wide and two feet long and weigh about 3 ½ pounds.

- Females of my kind usually weigh about 25% more than males.

- I eat mostly small rodents like mice, chipmunks, squirrels, voles, and bats. I also eat snakes and lizards and birds such as waterfowl, pigeons, quail, and occasional poultry.

- I like to sit on top of poles or in trees, watching for prey.

- My range extends from Alaska to Panama.

- I can easily be trained to hunt small game for people.

- I can soar to great heights and I flap my wings slowly and not very often.

- I usually fly about 40 miles per hour, but can dive as fast as 120 miles per hour!

- When full-grown, I have a reddish-brown tail with a pinkish underside.

RED-TAILED HAWK

What animal am I?

- I dig deep burrows in the beach sand of the intertidal zone.

- My burrows consist of long shafts leading to an enlarged chamber. There are usually two entrances.

- I will eat just about any animal I can overcome, including baby sea turtles. I also eat sea turtle eggs, clams, crabs, and carrion.

- My eyes are on top of tall stalks.

- I can breathe air if I keep my gills wet with sea water. However, I will drown if I stay underwater very long.

- I stay in my burrow during the heat of the day and during the coldest parts of winter.

- I have two large claws, one of which is larger than the other.

- Besides my claws, I have eight legs for walking. I move slowly with all eight legs, faster when I use six legs, and fastest when I use only four legs.

- I am most active at night.

- My eggs are laid in the sea and I spend the first part on my life as plankton before moving to live on land.

- I can slowly change color to match my surroundings or the time of day.

GHOST CRAB

What animal am I?

- I am about three quarters of inch long when full-grown.

- I am usually brownish gray and have brown stripes running down my body.

- I live in bushes, weeds, and grass. I am also found on rock walls, in ivy and other groundcover, and in buildings.

- Even though I have eight eyes, I have very poor vision.

- I am a fast runner and use my speed to catch my prey.

- I eat a wide variety of insects. They are paralyzed after my venomous bite.

- I am not dangerous to people, but my bite may cause some discomfort and swelling or redness.

- In the fall, our females crawl under rocks and logs and produce disk-shaped egg sacs. Then they die, still holding on to their eggs.

- Only our eggs are able to survive the winter.

- I live in a funnel–shaped web that is not sticky.

- My home is more easily seen when there is morning dew on the ground.

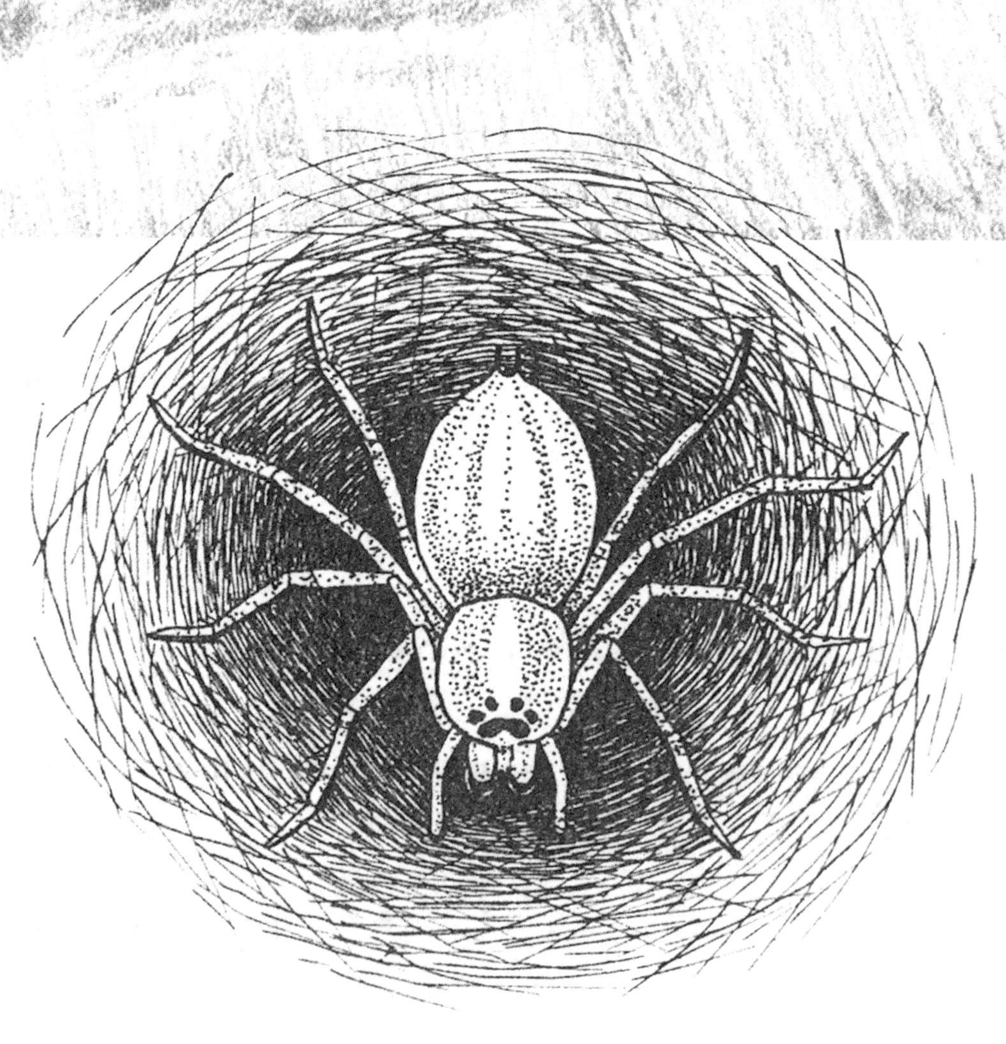

GRASS SPIDER

What animal am I?

- I have a reddish-brown body and wings and very long legs when I am grown. I am about 2/3 of an inch long.

- I like to build my nest under the eaves and on the ceilings of houses, barns, and other buildings.

- Our nests are made of chewed up wood and are light, tough, and strong. They usually have up to 150 chambers, or cells, all in one layer.

- Our females lay eggs in the cells of the nest, where they will hatch and grow into adults. If the egg is unfertilized, it will become a male.

- I feed in meadows, gardens, and fields on nectar and pollen from flowers and on juices from rotting fruits.

- I kill and chew up insects and feed them to the young in the nest.

- Our nests are attached to structures by just one narrow stalk that we coat with a chemical insect repellent.

- Only young mated females survive the winter each year, hiding in leaf litter or in stone crevices. They will begin a new nest the following spring.

- My main predators are birds.

PAPER WASP (with nest)

What animal am I?

- I usually mate for life.

- Both fathers and mothers regurgitate food to feed their young.

- I vary from black to gray to white in color.

- I usually hunt in groups of as many as 15.

- We often use the same trails over and over again.

- I eat whatever I can get, but prefer birds and mammals, including deer, caribou, and even moose. I will also eat insects, berries, and fish.

- I normally weigh between 60 and 130 pounds when full-grown.

- I live in remote forests and tundra.

- My life span is usually between 10 and 18 years.

- I am very vocal and speak in whimpers, growls, yelps, whines, barks, and howls. We respond to each other and also howl in unison.

GRAY WOLF

What animal am I?

- I am about one inch long when grown and shiny black, though I look bluish in the sunlight.

- I don't mind the presence of people and am not aggressive towards them.

- My main predator is the small bird known as the Tufted Titmouse.

- Males of my kind will stand guard over a nest, repelling intruders, parasites, and other males.

- My unfertilized eggs will become males and fertilized eggs will become females.

- Adults will feed the young born from fertilized eggs more food, so adult females are larger than adult males.

- Our nests consist of long parallel mud tubes containing cells where our eggs are laid.

- We provision our nests with paralyzed spiders to feed our young.

- We build nests on vertical surfaces in buildings, on rock faces, in hollow trees, and underneath bridges where they won't get rained on.

- When our young are full grown, they break out of the mud chambers and leave round holes where they emerged.

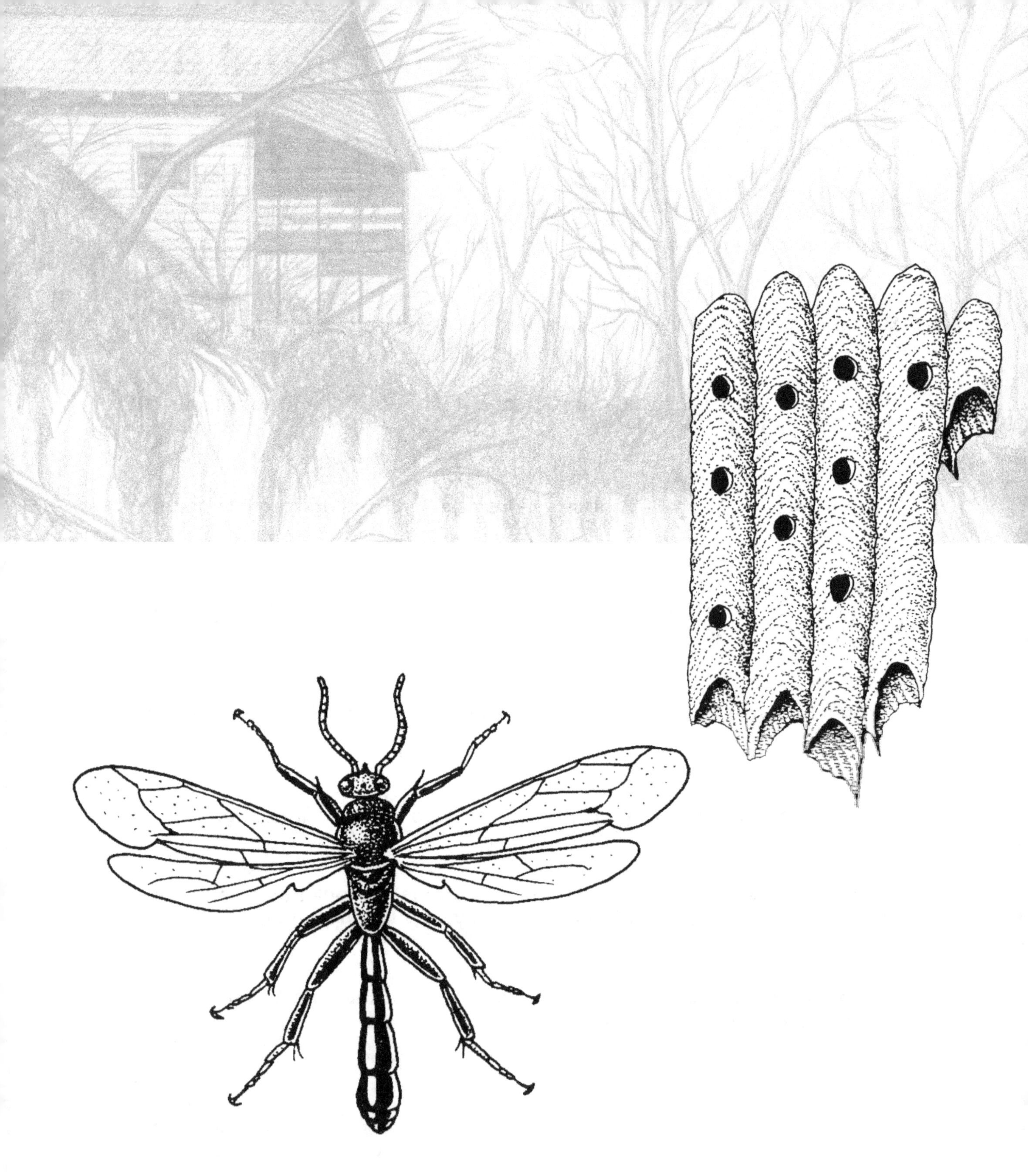

ORGAN-PIPE MUD DAUBER WASP (with nest)

What animal am I?

- I eat almost anything that is edible. However, I favor rodents and rabbits and I will occasionally attack livestock, such as sheep and calves.

- I weigh up to 55 pounds when full-grown, but normally weigh between 20 and 40 pounds.

- I am usually gray, with reddish, yellowish, and tan areas.

- I live on prairies, deserts, open woodlands, and brushy areas.

- I am most active at night.

- I can run more than 40 miles per hour!

- Sometimes, I travel long distances – journeys of 400 miles have been recorded.

- My babies are born in the spring. I have an average of seven babies at a time – but can have as many as 19!

- I sometimes live to be 18 years old in captivity, but 6 to 14 years in normal in the wild.

- My enemies are bears, mountain lions, wolves, and humans.

- I like to sing in the morning, evening, and at night in a series of high-pitched squeals and yaps. Other members of my group usually join me in song.

COYOTE

What animal am I?

- I am grayish brown with a pinkish bill when I am young.

- As an adult, I am almost completely white, with a black bill and feet and often with a yellow spot in front of my eyes.

- I am three feet long and seven feet wide when mature and can weigh as much as 21 pounds.

- I lay four to six white eggs on nests made of moss and grass near the water's edge.

- I live in the tundra, but spend the winter in shallow freshwater lakes and saltwater bays.

- When migrating, I fly during the day and night in V-shaped flocks of up to several hundred individuals.

- My main predators are foxes, eagles, bears, and wolves.

- In the summer I eat aquatic vegetation like eel-grass and sometimes grass on dry land. In the winter, I eat grains and leftover crops in farmers' fields, like potatoes.

- I have a very long neck which I hold straight up when swimming.

- My average life span is 10 years in the wild.

- My voice is like a muffled whistle.

WHISTLING SWAN

What animal am I?

- I live in swamps, thickets, and forests.

- My food is soft vegetation like grass and berries in the summer and twigs, bark, and conifer buds in the winter. I also eat carrion when I can find it.

- When being chased, I often run in circles, with speeds up to 30 miles per hour.

- I am dark brown in the summer, but I usually turn white in the autumn – even if I stay in a warm place. However, my hairs stay brown near my skin.

- I have large feet that enable me to walk on snow!

- I can have up to three litters per year.

- My population numbers vary dramatically from very high to very low in cycles of 9 or 10 years.

- I like to take baths in dust.

- I have many predators, including minks, weasels, bobcats, wolverines, lynxes, foxes, owls, and hawks.

- I often rest in hollow logs or burrows made by other animals – I don't make dens of my own.

- I weigh up to five pounds and am about 20 inches long. My ears are longer than my tail.

SNOWSHOE HARE

Index of Animals

Beaver

White-tailed
Deer

Raccoon

Star-nosed
Mole

Bobcat

Marsh
Rabbit

Gray Fox

Black Bear

TURTLE CROSSING

———

FOSSIL BEACH

———

VIRGINIA THROUGH TIME: A NATURAL HISTORY ATLAS

———

ANIMAL OBITUARIES

———

ANCIENT ANIMALS AND THEIR COINS

———

P. B.'s QUICK INDEX TO GAME FISH IN THE CHESAPEAKE BAY

———

FOSSIL DREAMS

———

ROMAN EMPRESSES

———

FOSSIL COLLECTING IN THE MID-ATLANTIC STATES

———

SELECTED LIVES

———

Many other titles on a variety of subjects